S0-AYZ-267

HOUSE DESIGN

daab

In recent years the lines that define the characteristics of the modern house have lost the severity that distinguished them in the past. Although the uses that a home must fulfill – cooking, relaxation, personal hygiene, interaction with other people, etc. – remain the same as ever, the solutions for tackling them are now very different and diverse. As a result, no specific formula can be established to define how a home should be. A house is conceived – and drawn up – with many considerations in mind. Adaptation to the terrain and the climate, the budget and the needs of its future inhabitants are all elements that affect its eventual form, but they are not definitive; an architect can use different strategies to resolve identical programs. Thus, some homes combine all their uses in a single space, while others separate the day-time and night-time areas, or those for work and leisure. Sometimes a project is understood as a continuum of its setting, in that a garden or terrace seems to become an additional room; in contrast, on other occasions a garden is treated as a natural exterior and windows with extensive perspectives are inserted in order to frame the landscape. The degree of differentiation is equally important when dealing with stories. In some residences every floor defines a use, while in others the staircase is the vertical axis that intercommunicates the entire house. The infinite diversity of solutions is especially striking in the home's three indispensable areas the kitchen, bedroom and bathroom. This analysis reveals cases in which the kitchen has been reduced to one piece of furniture that combines a refrigerator, cooker and microwave, set in a space that serves as both lounge and dining room, while at other times the kitchen's function is spread over two spaces, one for preparing food, the other an office that serves both for eating and storing utensils and foodstuffs. The function of resting has been distributed all over the home and, although the bed is normally placed in a room designed for privacy, it can also be found next to the lounge or in a space fitted with interior windows giving on to the dining room. Furthermore, recent innovations have made couches more comfortable than ever, and this offers the possibility of resting in the sitting room. Finally, the bathroom can be either a functional space set apart or it can occupy a privileged spot alongside the garden, with large windows, or spread itself out inside the house to such an extent that the bathtub turns into an indoor swimming pool.

Die Frage: „Was ist ein Haus?" lässt sich heutzutage nicht eindeutig beantworten. Auch wenn ein Wohnhaus dieselben Ansprüche wie eh und je zu erfüllen hat, d.h. es muss Raum zum Kochen, Schlafen, Waschen und Kommunizieren bieten, so wird diesen Wünschen doch auf vielseitige und ganz unterschiedliche Art Genüge getan. Von einer einheitlichen Definition, die genau festlegt, wie ein Zuhause auszusehen hat, sollten wir also Abstand nehmen. Ein Haus muss unter Berücksichtigung zahlreicher Gesichtspunkte entworfen werden. Die Anpassung des Hauses an Klima und Landschaft seines Standortes sowie die finanziellen Mittel und Bedürfnisse der zukünftigen Bewohner sind entscheidende aber nicht endgültige Kriterien seiner Gestaltung. Ein Architekt kann mit unterschiedlichen Strategien dieselben Konzepte verwirklichen. In einigen Häusern verteilt sich der gesamte Lebensraum auf ein einziges Ambiente, während in anderen eine Teilung zwischen Wohn- und Schlafräume oder Wohn- und Arbeitsbereich vorgenommen wird. Ein Haus kann in seine natürliche Umgebung übergehen, wobei sich der Garten oder die Terrasse als ein zusätzlicher Wohnraum konzipiert. Andererseits kann ein Haus sich eindeutig von der Landschaft abgrenzen. Der Garten wird hier als ein Äußeres erfahren und die Landschaft durch große Fensterfronten ausgegrenzt. Auch die innere Unterteilung eines Hauses ist wichtig. In einigen Häusern z.B. besitzt jedes Stockwerk eine unterschiedliche Funktion, während in anderen die Treppe als vertikale Achse alle unterschiedlichen Raumebenen miteinander verbindet. Die unendliche Vielfältigkeit von Wohngestaltung wird sichtbar, wenn man sich die unterschiedliche Gestaltung der drei elementaren Lebensbereiche eines Hauses wie die Küche, das Bad und das Schlafzimmer vor Augen hält: Während sich in einigen Häusern die Küche auf ein einziges Möbelstück reduziert, das Kühlschrank, Spüle und Mikrowelle miteinander vereint, erstreckt sich anderswo die Küche über zwei Räume, nämlich Küche und Esszimmer, bzw. Speisekammer. Schlafmöglichkeiten finden sich überall im Haus. Auch wenn das Bett normalerweise in einem abgegrenzten Raum steht, so kann sich dieser durchaus gleich neben dem Eingangsflur befinden oder durch Innenverglasung mit dem Esszimmer in Verbindung stehen. Doch auch im Wohnzimmer findet sich auf einem der bequemen Sofas immer Gelegenheit zum Ausruhen. Auch das Badezimmer präsentiert sich in vielfältigen Variationen: hier ein abgeschiedener funktionaler Ort, dort ein mit großen Fenstern ausgestattetes Zimmer mit Blick auf den Garten oder als enormer Baderaum, dessen Badewanne sich in ein Schwimmbad verwandelt hat.

Les lignes de définition typologique de la maison contemporaine ont récemment perdu leur gravité passée. Bien que les usages devant être satisfaits par une demeure – cuisiner, se reposer, faire sa toilette, sociali-ser…– demeurent immuables, les solutions permettant d'y répondre sont nombreuses et très distinctes. Il n'est ainsi pas possible d'établir une formule concrète établissant comment doit être un foyer.

La maison se pense – et se projette – en tenant compte de plusieurs axes directeurs. L'adaptation au terrain et au climat, le budget, les impératifs de ses futurs habitants sont des éléments marquant la forme finale, mais ils ne sont aucunement définitifs. Un architecte peut adopter des stratégies différentes pour répondre à des programmes pourtant identiques. De là des demeures englobant en un espace unique tous les usages, et d'autres séparant les zones diurnes et nocturnes, celles vouées au travail et aux loisirs. Parfois, un projet est compris comme un continuum au sein de l'environnement, de sorte que le jardin ou la terrasse deviennent une pièce de plus. En revanche, d'autres exemples traitent ce jardin comme un élément extérieur naturel et projettent des baies offrant de vastes perspectives encadrant les paysages.

Pour les appartements, le degré de différenciation est tout aussi crucial. Dans certaines résidences, chaque niveau définit un usage. Pour d'autres, l'escalier constitue l'axe vertical assurant les communications internes du lieu. L'infinie diversité des solutions s'apprécie surtout en observant les trois zones indispensables d'une demeure : la cuisine, la chambre et le bain. Cette analyse révèle des cas pour lesquels la cuisine se réduit à un meuble – accueillant réfrigérateur, cuisinière et micro-onde – situé dans un espace à la fois salon et salle à manger. Mais, dans d'autres occasion, cette fonction s'étend à deux espaces, l'un participant de l'élaboration du repas et l'autre, un office, servant tantôt à la déguster, tantôt à conserver les ustensiles et les aliments. La fonction de repos envahit, elle, tout le lieu. Ainsi, bien que le lit se trouve normalement dans une chambre, préservant l'intimité, celle-ci peut s'inviter à côté du hall d'entrée ou présenter des fenêtres intérieures don-nant sur la salle à manger. D'autre part, les innovations en matière de sofas les ont rendu toujours plus confor-tables. De là une possibilité de trouver le repos dans le salon de la maison. Enfin, le bain peut soit s'afficher comme une pièce purement fonctionnelle et séparée, soit occuper un lieu privilégié, mitoyen avec le jardin, voire s'étendre dans la maison, la baignoire devenue piscine intérieure.

Las líneas que definen la tipología de la casa actual han perdido la severidad que la distinguían en un pasado. Aunque los usos que debe satisfacer una vivienda –cocinar, descansar, asearse, relacionarse...– siguen siendo los de siempre, las soluciones para afrontarlos son muchos y muy distintos. Así, pues, no puede establecerse ninguna fórmula concreta que defina cómo debe ser un hogar.

La casa se piensa –y se proyecta– teniendo en cuenta múltiples directrices. La adaptación al terreno y al clima, el presupuesto o las necesidades de sus futuros habitantes son elementos que condicionan la forma que tendrá, pero no son definitivos; un arquitecto puede utilizar distintas estrategias para solventar programas idénticos. Así, hay viviendas que engloban en un único espacio todos los usos, mientras que otras separan las zonas diurnas y nocturnas o la del trabajo y del ocio. A veces un proyecto se entiende como la continuación del entorno, de manera que el jardín o la terraza devienen una habitación más; en cambio, otras veces se trata el jardín como un exterior natural y se diseñan ventanas de grandes perspectivas que encierran paisajes.

En lo que a pisos se refiere, el grado de diferenciación es igualmente importante. En algunas residencias, cada planta define un uso; en otras, la escalera es el eje vertical que comunica toda la casa. La infinita diversidad de soluciones se aprecia sobre todo al observar las tres zonas indispensables de una vivienda, es decir, la cocina, el dormitorio y el baño. Este análisis revela casos en los que la cocina ha quedado reducida a un mueble –que aúna nevera, fogón y microondas– ubicado en un espacio que es tanto salón como comedor, mientras que en otras ocasiones esta función se extiende a dos espacios, uno para elaborar la comida y una antecocina que sirve tanto para degustarla como de almacén de utensilios y alimentos. La función de descanso ha quedado distribuida por toda la casa, y aunque normalmente la cama se sitúa en una habitación que busca intimidad, esta puede encontrarse junto al recibidor o bien presentar ventanas interiores que den al comedor. Por otra parte, las innovaciones en los sofás los han convertido en piezas confortables y, por tanto, ofrecen la posibilidad de descansar en el salón de la casa. Por último, el baño puede ser tanto una pieza funcional y apartada como ocupar un lugar preferente al lado del jardín, con amplios ventanales, o expandirse dentro de la vivienda hasta que la bañera se convierte en una piscina interior.

Le linee che definiscono la tipologia della casa attuale hanno perso negli ultimi tempi l'antica severitá. Anche se le necessità che deve soddisfare un alloggio –poter cucinare, riposarsi, lavarsi, stabilire relazioni, ecc.- continuano ad essere quelle di sempre, le soluzioni per affrontarle sono molte e molto diverse. Dunque non è possibile stabilire nessuna formula concreta che definisca come deve essere un'abitazione.

La casa viene pensata – e progettata - tenendo in considerazione molteplici direttrici. L'adeguamento al terreno e al clima, il preventivo, le necessità dei futuri abitanti, sono elementi che indicano la forma che avrà, ma non la definiscono: un architetto può utilizzare strategie diverse per risolvere identici schemi. Così ci sono alloggi che inglobano in un unico spazio tutti gli usi, mentre altri separano gli spazi in zona giono e zona notte, o in spazi di lavoro e di ozio. A volte un progetto viene inteso come un continuum dell'ambiente circostante, di modo che il giardino o la terrazza divengono una stanza in più; altre volte il giardino viene trattato come un esterno naturale e vengono progettate finestre a grandi vedute che ne rinchiudono il paesaggio.

Per ciò che si riferisce agli appartamenti il grado di differenziazione è ugualmente importante. In alcuni edifici ogni piano definisce un uso, in altri la scala è l'asse verticale che mette in comunicazione tutto l'alloggio. L'infinita diversità di soluzioni si apprezza soprattutto osservando le tre zone indispensabili di un'abitazione, cioè la cucina, la stanza da letto ed il bagno. Quest'analisi rivela casi nei quali la cucina è stata ridotta ad un mobile – che riunisce frigorifero, fuochi e microonde - situato in uno spazio che è sia soggiorno che pranzo, mentre in altre occasioni questa funzione si sviluppa in due spazi, uno per elaborare i pasti ed un office che serve sia per degustarli che per il deposito degli utensili e degli alimenti. La funzione del riposare viene distribuita in tutta la casa, ed anche se normalmente il letto viene collocato in una camera in cerca di privacy, la si può trovare situata vicino all'ingresso o può avere finestre interne che affacciano sul pranzo. D'altra parte, le novità nel settore divani li ha resi sempre più confortevoli e questo offre la possibilità di riposare nel soggioro di casa. Per ultimo il bagno può essere sia un vano funzionale ed appartato, o può occupare un luogo privilegiato al lato del giardino, con grandi vetrate, o addirittura espandersi dentro la casa al punto che la vasca si trasformi in una piscina interna.

4SITE | SYDNEY
LANE + STUMM RESIDENCE
Sydney, Australia | 2000

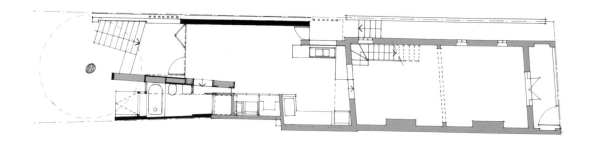

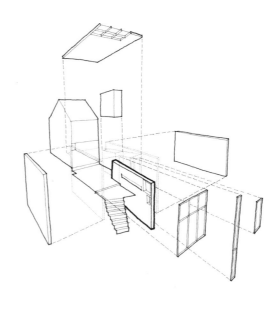

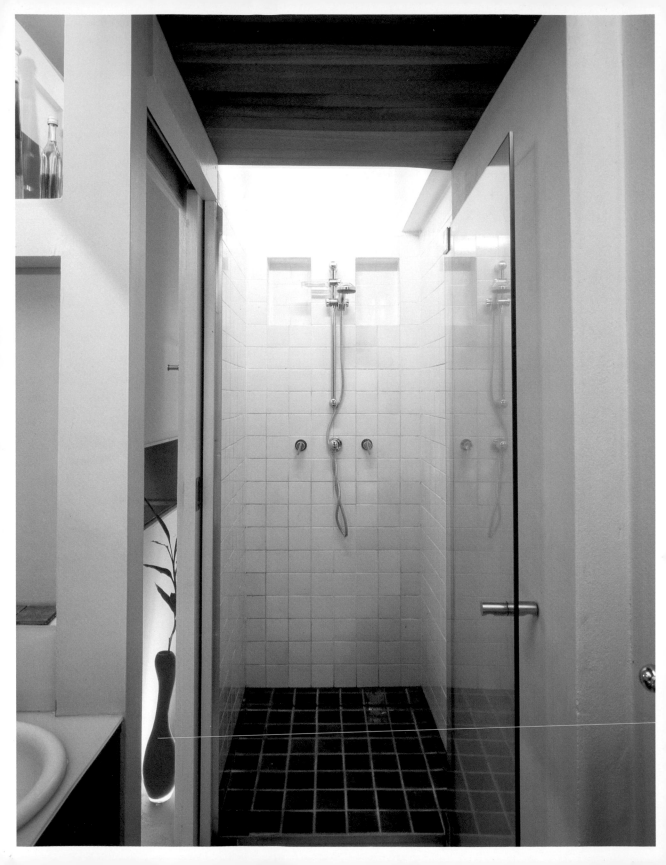

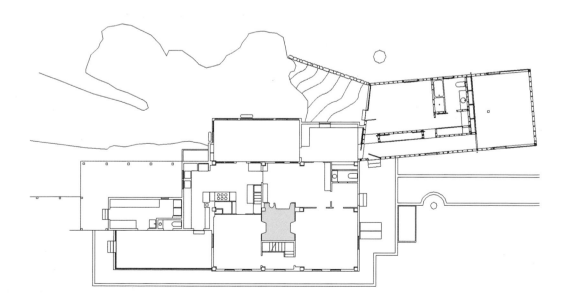

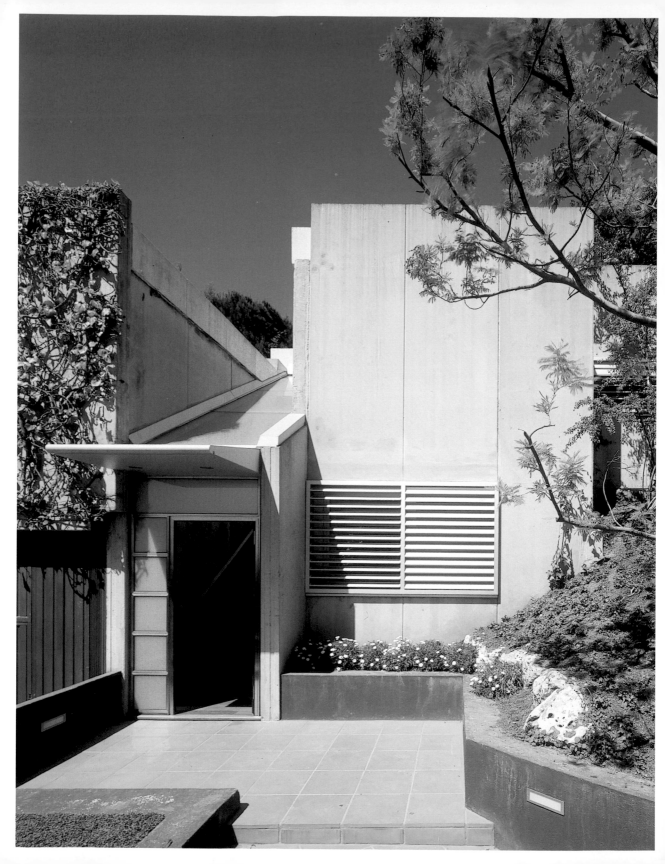

ANTONI PUIG, GCA ARQUITECTES ASSOCIATS | BARCELONA
PUIG HOUSE
Barcelona, Spain | 2001

ARCHINAUTEN | LINZ
VILLA H
Linz, Austria | 2004

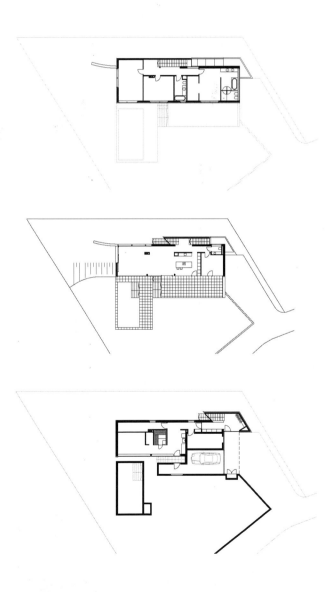

ARCHITEKTURWERKSTATT DWORZAK| DORNBIRN
SAGMEISTER HOUSE
Sibratsgfäll, Austria | 2002

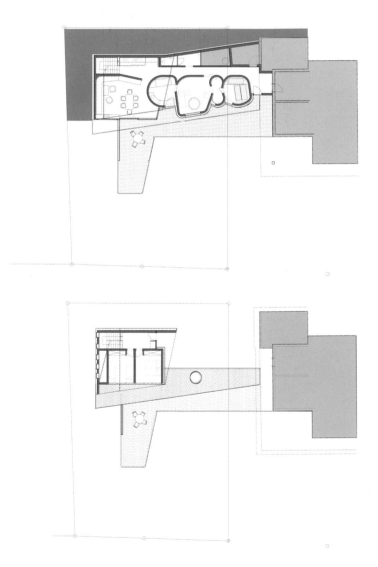

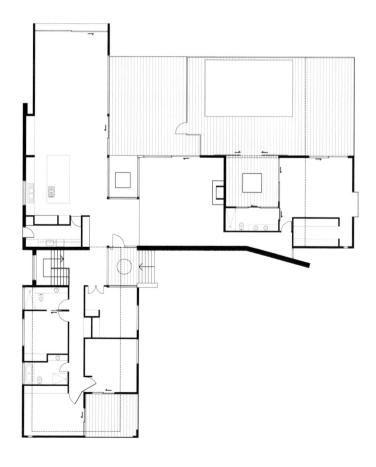

BFP ARQUITECTOS | BARCELONA
HOUSE IN FONTPINEDA
Pallejà, Spain | 2001

BFP ARQUITECTOS | BARCELONA
M. HOUSE
Alicante, Spain | 2001

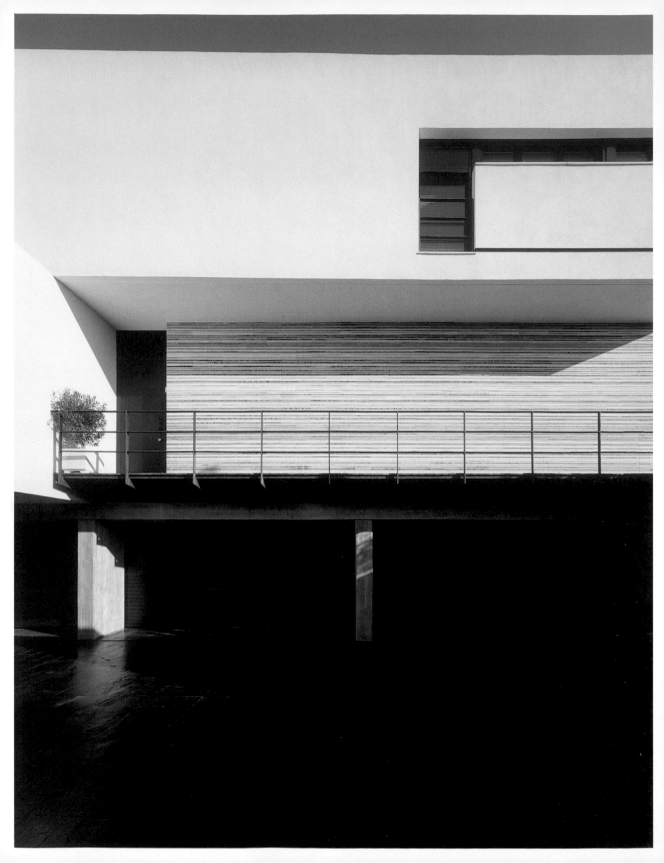

CARAMEL ARCHITEKTEN | **VIENNA**
HOUSE H
Linz, Austria | 2003

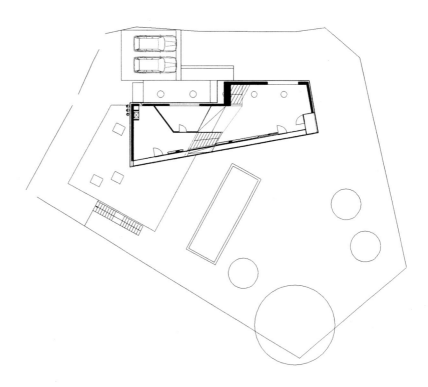

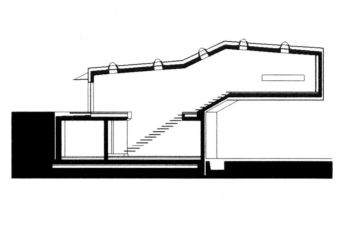

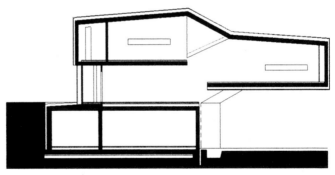

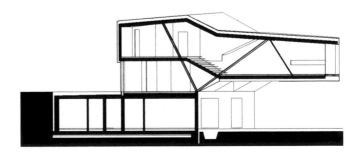

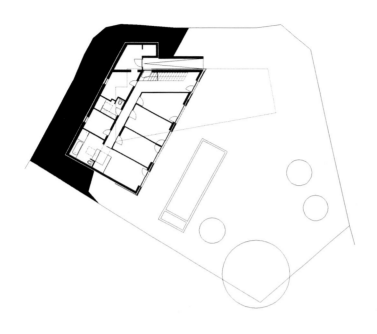

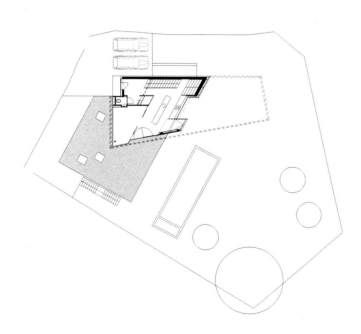

DAIGO ISHI FUTURE-SCAPE ARCHITECTS | TOKYO
COTTAGE C
Fushiguro Castle Campsite, Japan | 2000

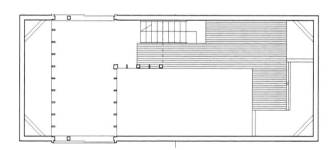

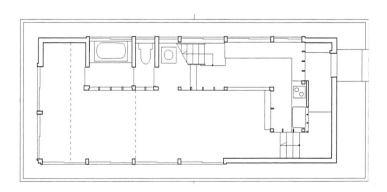

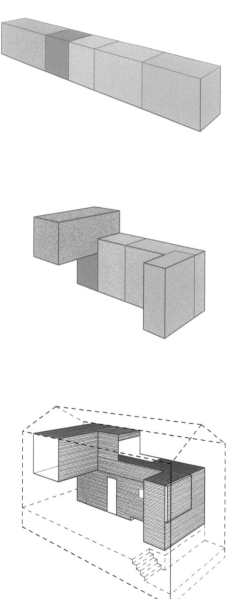

DAIGO ISHI FUTURE-SCAPE ARCHITECTS | TOKYO
HOUSE IN AIHARA
Aihara, Japan | 2002

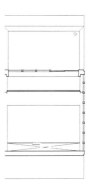

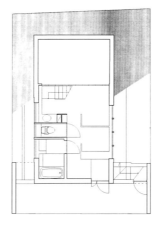

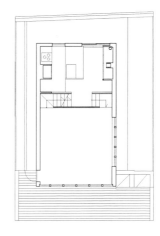

DIETRICH | UNTERTRIFALLER | BREGENZ
B. HOUSE
Klaus, Austria | 2003

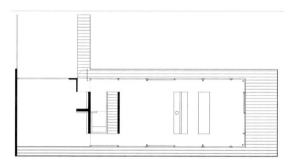

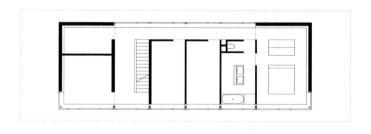

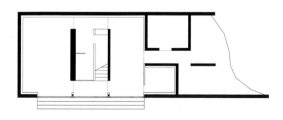

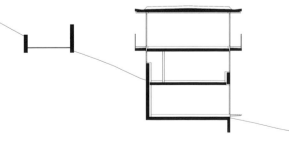

DIETRICH | UNTERTRIFALLER | BREGENZ

R. HOUSE
Bregenz, Austria | 2002

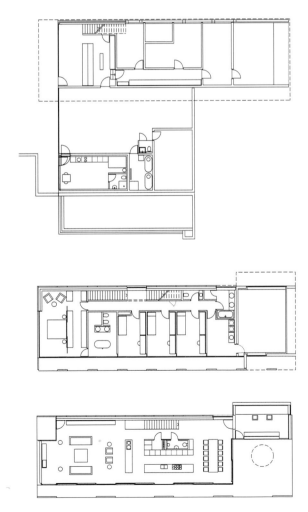

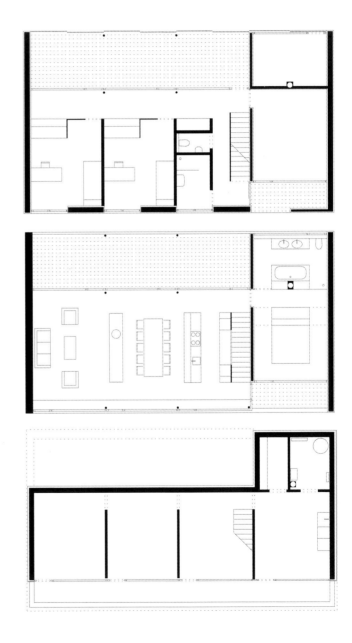

DÖRING DAHMEN JOERESSEN ARCHITEKTEN | DUSSELDORF

PANTHÖFER HOUSE
Meerbush, Germany | 2003

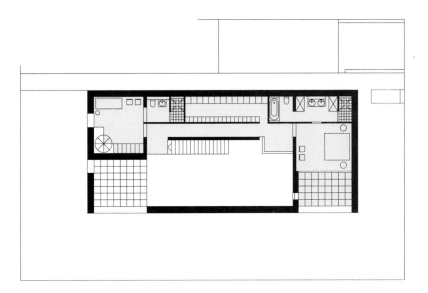

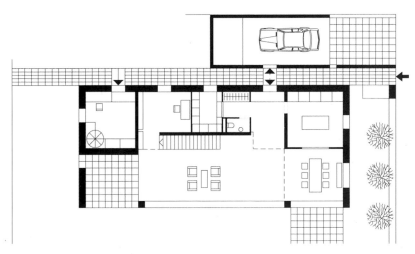

ERIC ROSEN ARCHITECTS | LOS ANGELES
FAIRWAIS RESIDENCE
Nashville, USA | 2000

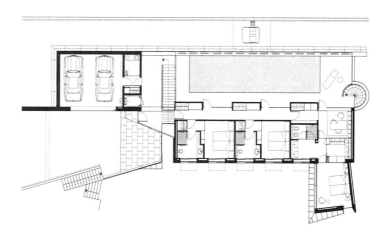

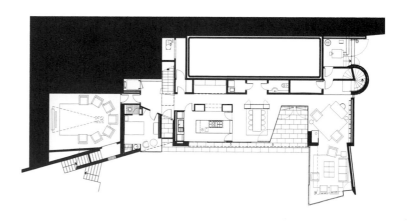

FELIPE ASSADI | SANTIAGO DE CHILE

RAVEAU HOUSE
Santiago de Chile, Chile | 2003

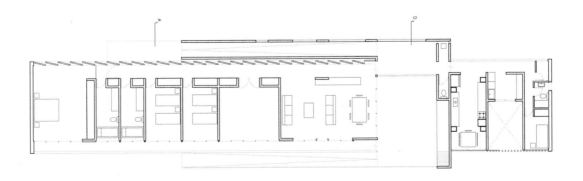

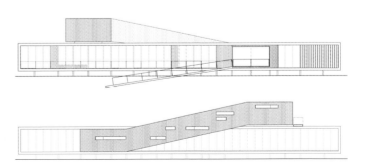

SUITCASE HOUSE
Badaling Shuiguan-Beijin, China | 2002

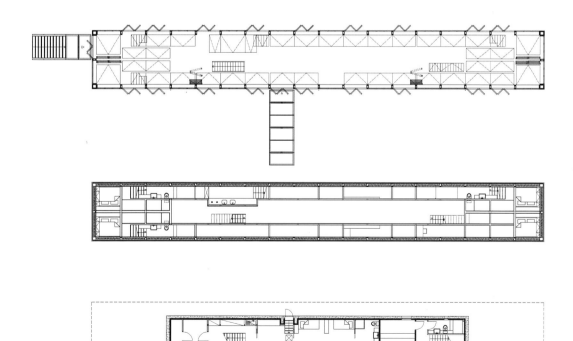

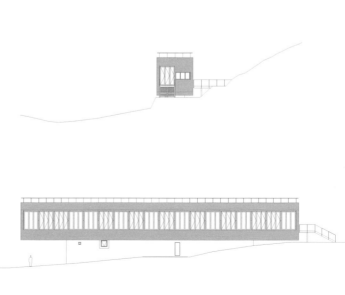

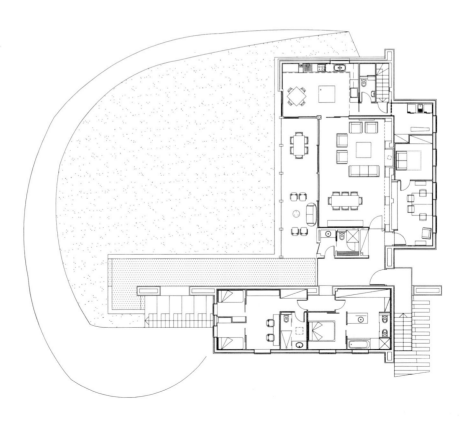

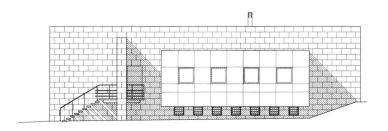

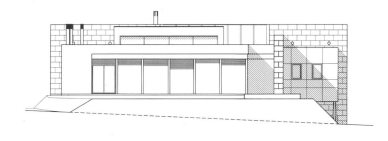

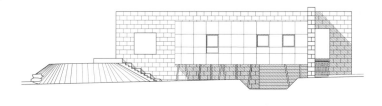

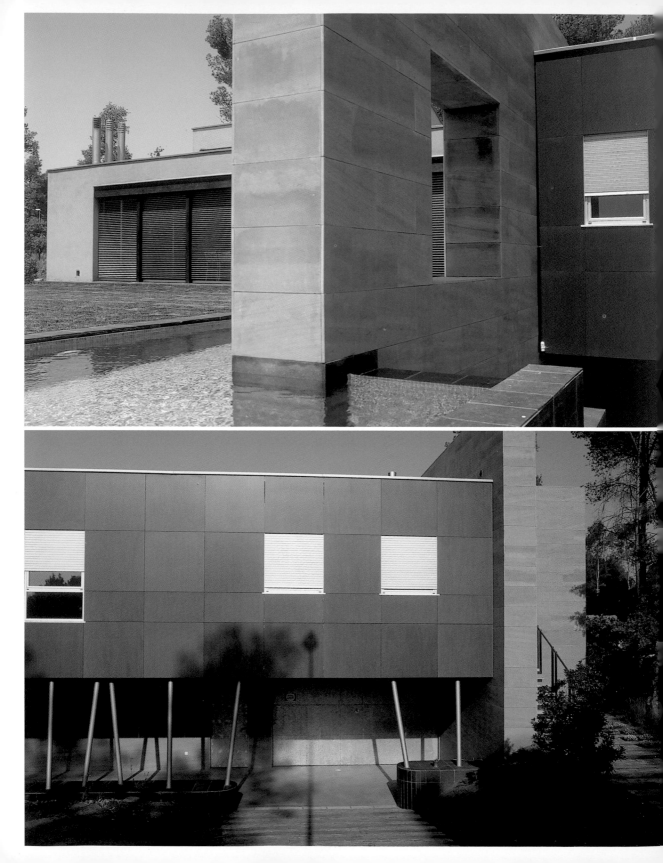

GRAFTWORKS ARCHITECTURE + DESIGN | NEW YORK

MOUNTAIN HOUSE
Stratton, USA | 2003

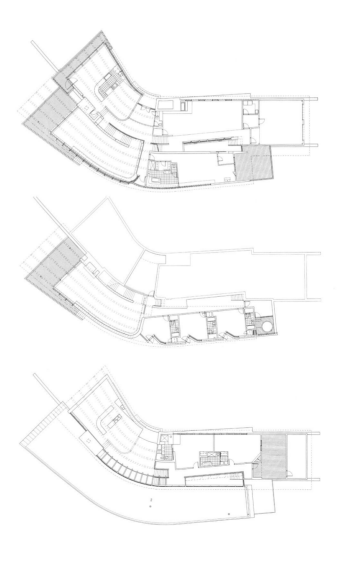

GROEP DELTA ARCHITECTUUR | HASSELT
VILLA C
Hasselt, Belgium | 2001

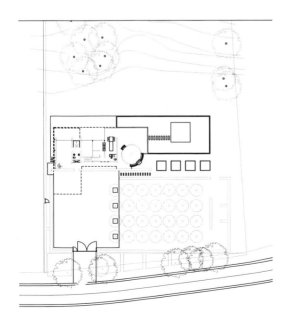

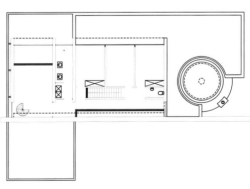

HERTL.ARCHITEKTEN | STEYR
STEINWENDTNER HOUSE
Steyr, Austria | 2003

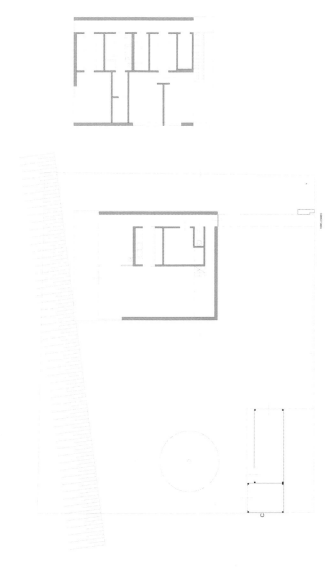

IVAN KROUPA ARCHITECTS | PRAGUE

BRIDGE HOUSE
Vitavou, Czech Republic | 2001

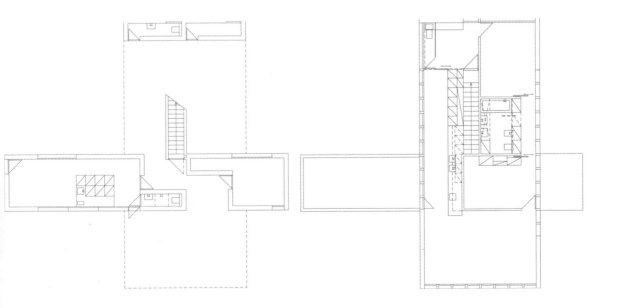

JAIME SANAHUJA, EMILIO CUBILLOS, JOSÉ Mª MEDRANO | CASTELLÓN
FRONT SEA HOUSE
Castellón, Spain | 2003

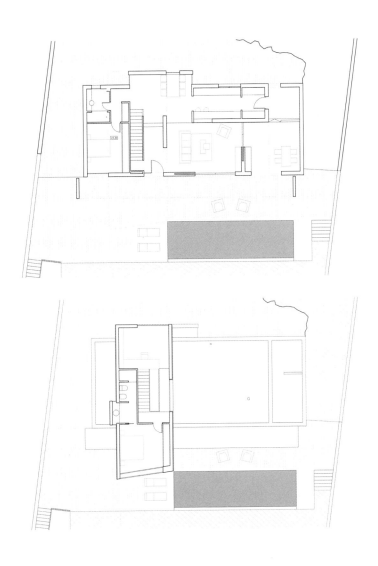

JAIME SANAHUJA, EMILIO CUBILLOS, JOSÉ Mª MEDRANO | CASTELLÓN
VILLA +
Castellón, Spain | 2003

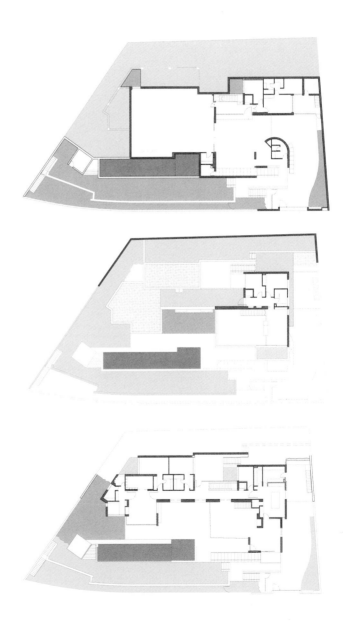

JORDI BIETO | BARCELONA
HOUSE IN TERRASA
Terrassa, Spain | 2001

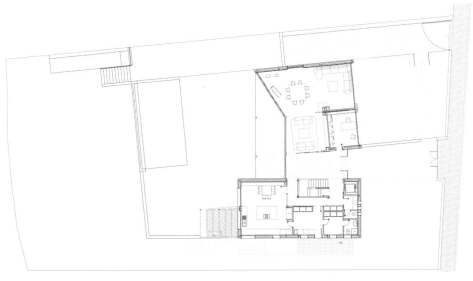

JOSEP Mª FONT, GREEK | BARCELONA
HOUSE IN ESPLUGUES
Esplugues del Llobregat, Spain | 2003

JURG GRASER, GRASER ARCHITEKTEN | ZURICH
HUBER HOUSE
Luzern, Switzerland | 2003

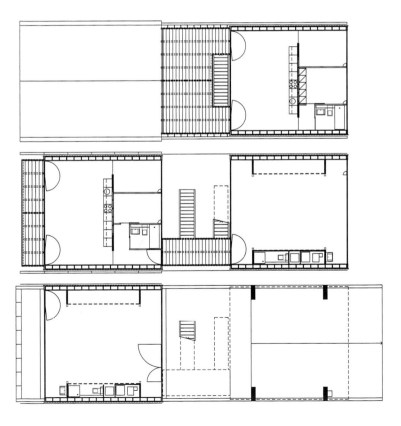

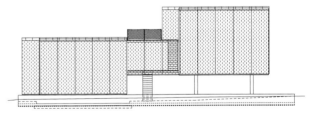

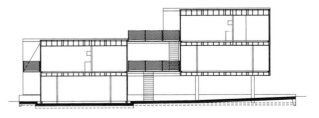

KAA KIRKPATRIK ASSOCIATES ARCHITECTS | LOS ANGELES

OCEAN DRIVE RESIDENCE
Manhattan Beach, USA | 2003

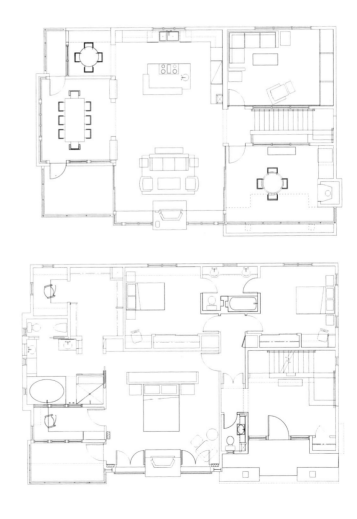

MAMEN DOMINGO ¡! ERNEST FERRÉ ARQUITECTES | BARCELONA

VILLA MAITE
Reus, Spain | 2000

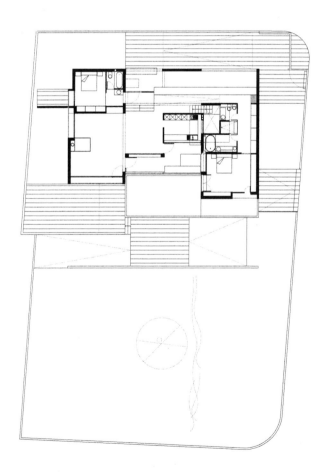

MANUELA GONZÁLEZ MOYA + JUAN JOSÉ PASTOR GARCÍA, ARQUITECTOS | NOVELDA
HOUSE IN NOVELDA
Novelda, Spain | 2003

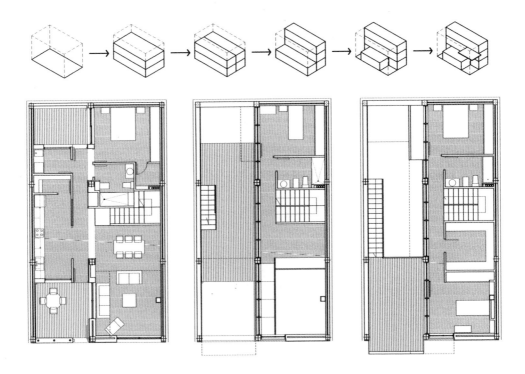

MATEU BARBA, JOSEP CARRETÉ, EDUARD MONTANÉ: SET ARQUITECTES | BARCELONA
TIH HOUSE
Barcelona, Spain | 2003

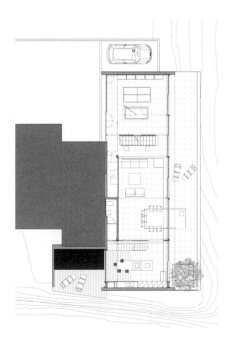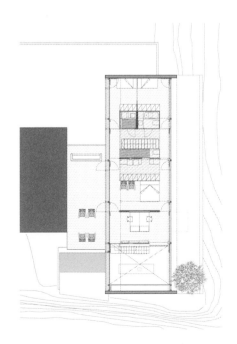

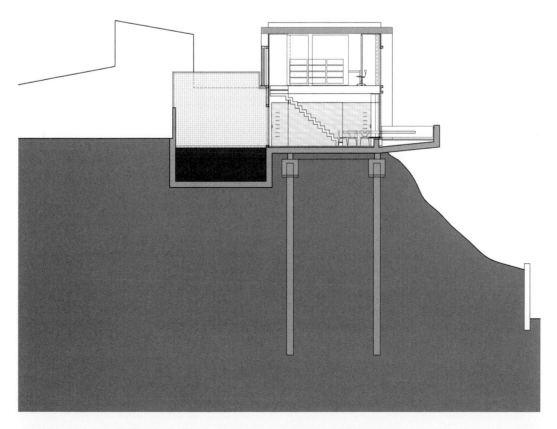

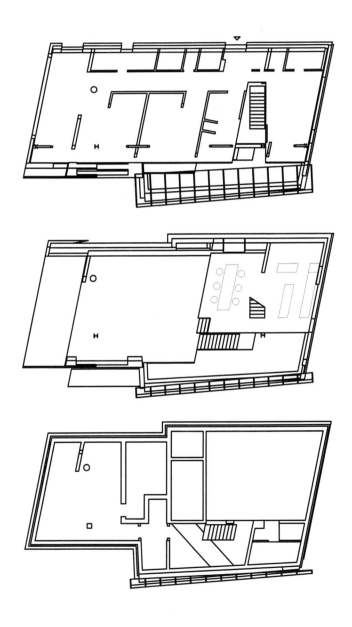

MUTSUE HAYAKUSA, CELL SPACE ARCHITECTS | TOKYO

KOUENJI HOUSE
Tokyo, Japan | 2003

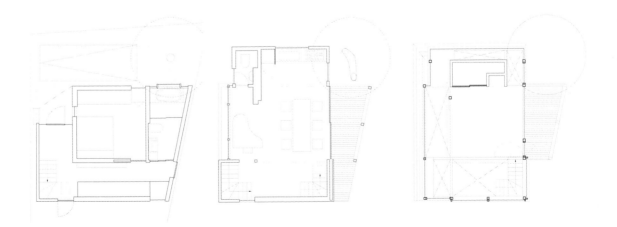

NAYA ARCHITECTS: MANABU + ARATA | KANAGAWA
FUTOKOSHINCHI HOUSE
Futakoshinchi, Japan | 2004

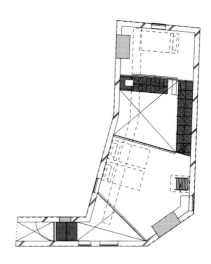

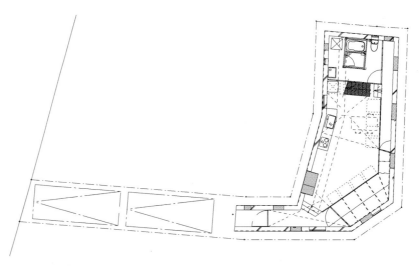

NAYA ARCHITECTS: MANABU + ARATA | KANAGAWA

TESHI HOUSE

Kawasaki-shi, Japan | 2003

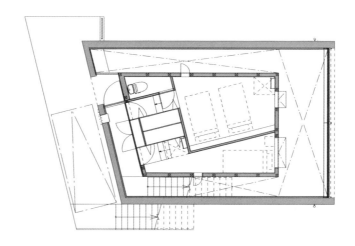

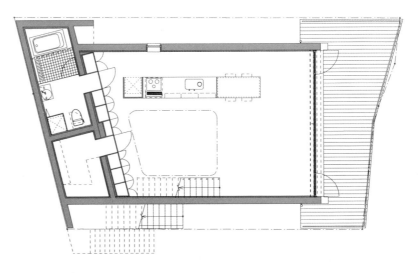

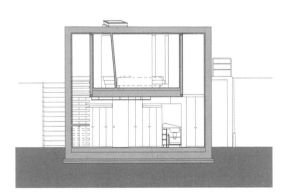

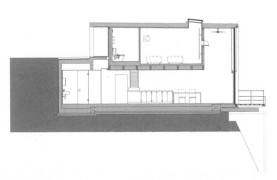

OISHI KAZUHIKO ARCHITECTURE ATELIER | FUKUOKA
CITY CUBE
Fukuoka, Japan | 2002

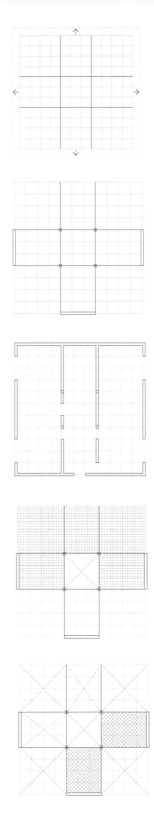

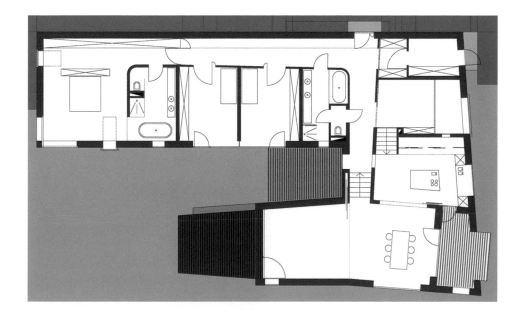

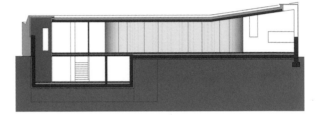

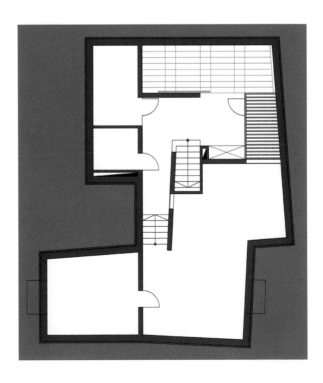

PICHLER & TRAUPMANN ARCHITEKTEN | VIENNA
HACKENBUCHNER HOUSE
Vienna, Austria | 2001

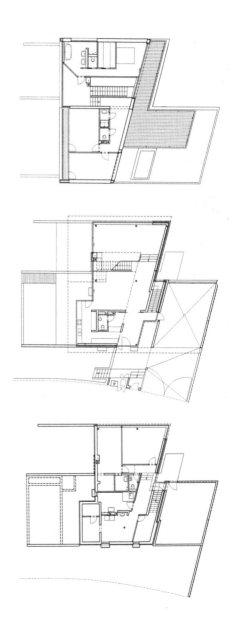

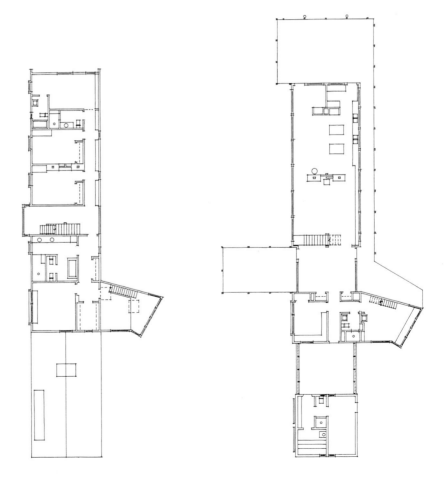

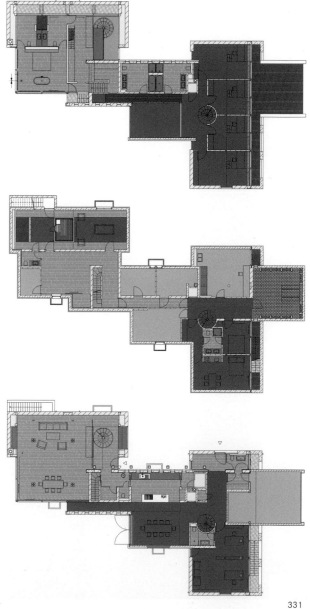

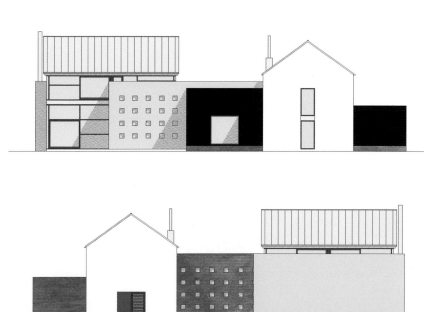

STÉPHANE BEEL ARCHITEKTEN | GENT
VILLA B
Brasschaat, Belgium | 1999

SUSANA ANDREA HERRERA. FACTORIA DESIGN | **CHILE**
ELIPSE HOUSE
Andalue, Chile | 2003

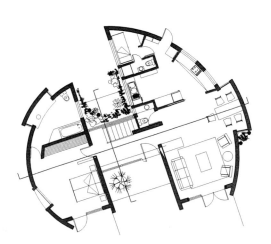
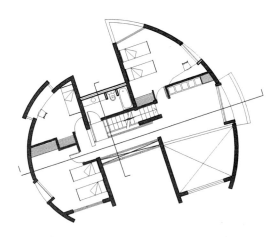

TATANKA IDEENVERTRIEBSGESELLSCHAFT | MILS
BAUMHAUSBERG HOUSE
Telfs, Austria | 2001

TITO DALMAU, BDM ARQUITECTOS (BRIONES-DALMAU-MARQUES) | BARCELONA
CASA DE LAS ALAS
Barcelona, Spain | 2001

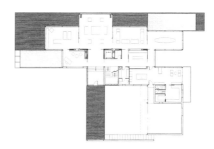

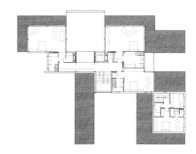

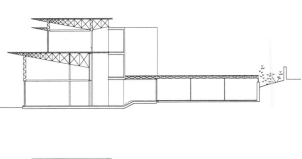

WOLFGANG FEYFERLIK AND SUSI FRITZER | GRAZ

HOUSE R
Graz, Austria | 2002

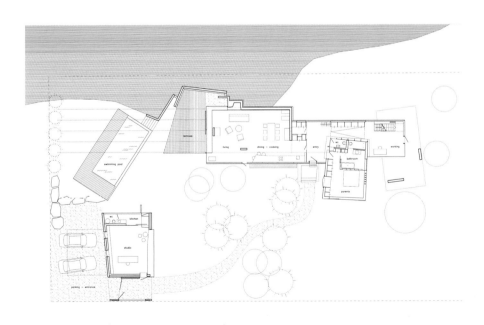

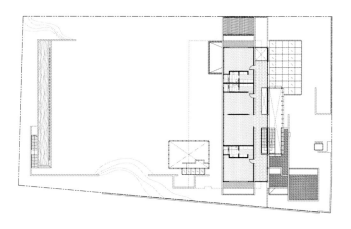

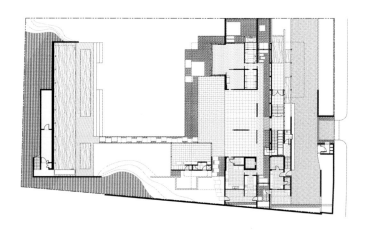

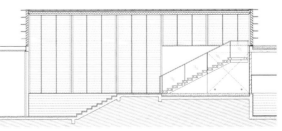

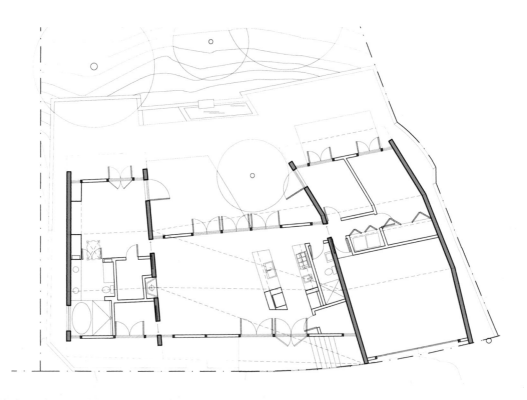

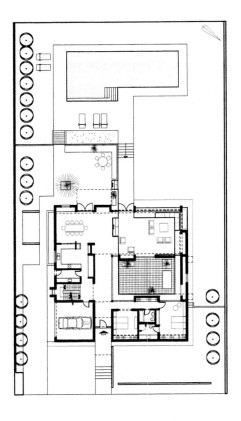

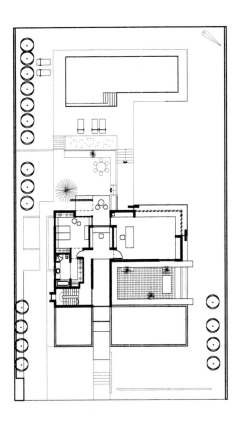

4Site
41 Bedford Street, North Melbourne 3051, Australia
P +61 4 0213 1147
F +61 3 9326 8481
peter-farman@4site-design.com
www.4site-design.com
Lane + Stumm Residence
Photos: © Tyrone Branigan

Andrew Berman Architect
77 Chambers Street, 10007 New York, USA
P +12 1 2226 5998
F +12 1 2226 5657
abarchitect@earthlink.net
www.andrewbermanarchitect.com
Wood House
Photos: © Catherine Tighe

Antoni Puig, GCA Arquitectes Associats
Valencia 289, bajos, 08009 Barcelona, Spain
P +34 93 476 18 00
F +34 93 476 18 06
info@gcaarq.com
www.gcaarq.com
Puig House
Photos: © Eugeni Pons

Archinauten
Schratzstrasse 11, 4040 Linz, Austria
P +43 7 071 052
F +43 7 071 058
office@archinauten.com
www.archinauten.com
Villa H
Photos: © Michael Dworschak

Architekturwerkstatt Dworzak
Steinebach 3, 6850 Dornbirn, Austria
P +43 5 5723 4228
F +43 5 5725 5583
hugo.dworzak@aon.at
www.austria-architects.com
Sagmeister House
Photos: © Ignacio Martínez

Atelier Oï
Signolet 3, 2520 La Neuveville, Switzerland
P +41 3 2751 5666
F +41 3 2751 5655
contact@atelier-oi.ch
www.atelier-oi.ch
Maison Monde
Photos: © Yves André

BBP Architects
7/25 Argyle St., Fitzroy, Victoria 3065, Australia
P +61 3 9416 1486
F +61 3 9416 1438
info@bbparchitects.com
www.bbparchitects.com
Portsea Residence
Photos: © Shania Shegedyn

BFP Arquitectos. Robin Perna
Vallirana 7, pral. 1ª, 08006 Barcelona
P +34 93 415 74 17
F +34 93 415 86 09
perna@coac.es
www.perna-arquitectos.com
House in Fontpineda
Photos: © Eugeni Pons
M. House
Photos: © Eugeni Pons

BFP Arquitectos. Pablo Beltrán and Alfonso Fernández
Pau Claris 173, 2° 1ª, 08037 Barcelona
P +34 93 487 93 41
F +34 93 487 93 42
beyfe@telefonica.net
House in Fontpineda
Photos: © Eugeni Pons
M. House
Photos: © Eugeni Pons

Caramel Architekten
Schlttenfeldeldgasse 72/2/3, 1070 Vienna, Austria
P +43 1 596 3490
F +43 1 596 3420
kha@caramel.at
www.caramel.at
House H
Photos: © Caramel

Daigo Ishi Future-scape Architects
Yahagi Building 401, 1-19-14, Yoyogi, Shibuya-ke,
151-0053 Tokyo, Japan
P +81 3 5350 0855
F +81 3 5350 0854
digodigo@ea.mbn.or.jp
Cottage C
Photos: © Future Scape Architects & The Japan Architect
House in Aihara
Photos: © Future Scape Architects & The Japan Architect

Dietrich I Untertrifaller
Albergstrasse 117, 6900 Bregenz, Austria
P +43 5 5747 8888
F +43 5 5747 8820
arch@dietrich.untertrifaller.com
www.dietrich.untertrifaller.com
B. House
Photos: © Ignacio Martínez
R. House
Photos: © Ignacio Martínez
S. House
Photos: © Ignacio Martínez

Döring Dahmen Joeressen Architekten
Hansaalle 321, 40549 Dusseldorf, Germany
P +49 2 1153 7553
F +49 2 1153 7575
info@ddj.de
www.ddj.de
Panthöfer House
Photos: © Manos Meisen

Eric Rosen Architects
11525 Washington Blvd, Los Angeles 90066, USA
P +13 1 0313 3052
F +13 1 0313 3062
thestudio@ericrosen.com
www.ericrosen.com
Fairwais Residence
Photos: © Eric Koyama

Espinet-Ubach Arquitectes i Associats
Camp 63, bajos, 08022 Barcelona, Spain
P +34 93 418 78 33
F +34 93 417 21 22
espinet-ubach@retemail.es
V. House
Photos: © Joan Mundó

Felipe Assadi
Málaga 940, 755-0388 Santiago de Chile, Chile
P +56 2 263 5738
F +56 2 207 6984
info@assadi.cl
www.felipeassadi.com
Raveau House
Photos: © Guy Wenborne

Gary Chan, Edge Design Institute
1706-08, 663 King's Road, North Point, Hong Kong, China
P +85 2 2802 6212
F +85 2 2802 6213
gary@edge.hk.com
www.edge.hk.com
Suitcase House
Photos: © Edge Design Institute

Gorina i Farrés Arquitectes
Pedregar 1° 3ª, 08202 Sabadell, Spain
P +34 93 745 16 80
Farrés-Alsina House
Photos: © Miquel Tres

Graftworks Architecture + Design
1123 Broadway, suite 715, New York 10010, USA
P +12 1 2366 9675
F +12 1 2366 9075
info@graftworks.net
www.graftworks.net
Mountain House
Photos: © David Joseph

Groep Delta Architectuur
Ilgatlaan 9, 3500 Hasselt, Belgium
P +32 1 128 4969
F +32 1 128 1185
info@groepdelta.com
www.groepdelta.com
Villa C
Photos: © Groep Delta Architectuur

Hertl.Architekten
Zwischenbrücken 4, 4400 Steyr, Austria
P +43 7 2524 6944
F +43 7 2524 7363
steyr@hertl-architekten.com
www.hertl-architekten.com
Steinwendtner House
Photos: © Paul Ott

Ivan Kroupa Architects
Goncarenkova 10, Prague 4, Czech Republic
P +42 7 2403 7808
F +42 2 4446 0103<<
ivankroupa@ivankroupa.cz
www.ivankroupa.cz
Bridge House
Photos: © Matteo Piazza

Jaime Sanahuja, Emilio Cubillos, José Mª Medrano
Fernando el Católico 34, 12005 Castellón, Spain
P +34 96 472 49 49
F +34 96 472 49 46
sanahuja@ctac.es
Front Sea House
Photos: © Joan Roig
Villa +
Photos: © Joan Roig

Jordi Bieto
Mercè Rodoreda, 08190 Sant Cugat del Vallés, Spain
P +34 93 589 86 72
F +34 93 590 31 11
jordibieto@teleonica.net
House in Terrassa
Photos: © Jovan Horváth

Josep Mª Font, Greek
Rubinstein 4, 08022 Barcelona, Spain
P +34 93 418 95 50
F +34 93 418 95 32
greek@greekbcn.com
www.greekbcn.com
House in Esplugues
Photos: © Nuria Fuentes

Jurg Graser, Graser Architekten
Neugasse 6, 8005 Zurich, Switzerland
P +41 4 3366 9900
F +41 4 3366 9901
architekten@graser.ch
www.graser.ch
Huber House
Photos: © Thomas Jantscher

KAA Kirkpatrik Associates Architects
4201 Redwood Avenue, Los Angeles 90066, USA
P +13 1 0821 1400
F +13 1 0821 1440
ecorvo@kaa-architects.com
www.kaa-architects.com
Ocean Drive Residence
Photos: © Weldon Brewster

Mamen Domingo ¡! Ernest Ferré Arquitectes
Diputació 239, 1° 2ª B, 08007 Barcelona, Spain
P +34 93 487 01 05
domingoferre@terra.es
www.domingoferre.com
Villa Maite
Photos: © Jovan Horváth

Manuela González Moya + Juan José Pastor García, Arquitectos
Maestro Ramis 17, bajos derecha, 03660 Novelda, Spain
P +34 9 6560 1848
F +34 9 6560 1848
zambra@teleline.es
House in Novelda
Photos: © David Frutoc Ruiz

Mateu Barba, Josep Carreté, Eduard Montané: Set Arquitectes
Provença 293, 4° 1ª, 08037 Barcelona, Spain
P +34 93 207 06 11
F +34 93 457 02 69
mateu_barba@coac.net
TIH House
Photos: © Eugeni Pons

Michael Haberz
Teichweg 11, 8075 Hart, Austria
P +43 3 1649 3800
F +43 3 1649 3800
arch.haberz@utanet.at
Haberz House
Photos: © Paul Ott

Mutsue Hayakusa, Cell Space Architects
3-12-3 Kugahara, Ohta-ku, 146-0085 Tokyo, Japan
P +81 3 5748 1011
F +81 3 5748 1012
mutsu@kt.rim.or.jp
www.cell-space.com
Kouenji House
Photos: © Hiroshi Ueda

Naya Architects: Manabu + Arata
Kamimaruko San-nocho 2-1376-1F
Nakahara-ku, Kawasaki-shi, 211-0002 Kanagawa, Japan
P +81 4 4411 7934
F +81 4 4411 7935
m-a.naya@f2.dion.ne.jp
www.f2.dion.ne.jp/~m-a.naya
Futokoshinchi House
Photos: © Koui Yaginuma / Title
Teshi House
Photos: © Makoto Yoshida

Oishi Kazuhiko Architecture Atelier
7-2-7 Nishijin, Sawara-ku, 814-0002 Fukuoka, Japan
P +81 9 2823 0882
F +81 9 2823 0925
kaz.oishi@jcom.home.ne.jp
www.members.jcom.home.ne.jp/oishi.architect
City Cube
Photos: © Kouji Okamoto

Peter Ebner and Franziska Ullmann
Windühlgasse 9/26, 1060 Vienna, Austria
P +43 1 586 8522
F +43 1 587 7887
ebner-ullmann@aon.at
House O
Photos: © Margherita Spiluttini

Pichler & Traupmann Architekten
Kundmanngasse 39/12, 1030 Vienna, Austria
P +43 1 713 3203
F +43 1 713 3213
pxt@vienna.at
Hackenbuchner House
Photos: © Paul Ott

Salmela Architect
852 Grandview Avenue, Duluth, Minnesota 55812, USA
P +12 1 8724 7517
F +12 1 8728 6805
ddsalmela@charter.net
Koehler Retreat
Photos: © Peter Bastianelli Kerze

Stadler + Partner
Balanstrasse 9, 81669 Munich, Germany
P +49 8 9489 2400
F +49 8 9448 7111
architekten@planungswelt.de
www.planungswelt.de
HS56 Singular Housing project
Photos: © Ullrich Grohs

Stéphane Beel Architekten
Kouter 1, 9000 Gent, Belgium
P +32 9 269 5150
F +32 9 269 5159
mail@stephanebeel
B. House
Photos: © Conrad White

Susana Andrea Herrera. Factoria Design
Chacabuco 774, 405-0030 Santiago de Chile, Chile
P +56 4 122 5561
susana@factoriadesign.com
www.factoriadesign.com
Elipse House
Photos: © José Luis Saavedra Morales

Tatanka Ideenvertriebsgesellschaft
Brunnholzstrasse 12a, 6068 Mils, Austria
P +43 5 2235 2202
F +43 5 2235 2218
architekten@tatanka.lu
Baumhausberg House
Photos: © Paul Ott

Tito Dalmau, BDM Arquitectos (Briones-Dalmau-Marques)
Passeig Picasso 12, 2° 2ª, 08003 Barcelona, Spain
P +34 93 319 68 90
F +34 93 319 40 90
bdmsc@coac.es
Casa de las Alas
Photos: © Tito Dalmau

Wolfgang Feyferlik and Susi Fritzer
Glacisstrasse 7, 8010 Graz, Austria
P +43 3 1634 7656
F +43 3 1638 6029
fritzer@inode.cc
House R
Photos: © Paul Ott

WOHA Designs
175 Telok Ayer Street, 068623 Singapore, Singapore
P +65 6 423 4555
F +65 6 423 4666
admin@wohadesigns.com
www.wohadesigns.com
Rochalie Drive Residence
Photos: © Tim Griffith

Xten Architecture
201 S. Santa Fe Avenue, suite 202, Los Angeles 90012, USA
P +12 1 3625 7002
F +12 1 3625 7004
mail@xtenarchitecture.com
www.xtenarchitecture.com
Vhouse
Photos: © Art Gray, Benny Chan Photoworks

Yoram Reisinger
3 Rama Street, 53320 Givatayim, Israel
P +97 2 3571 4982
F +97 2 3571 1695
yoram888@bezeqint.net
Reisinger House
Photos: © Yael Pincus

copyright © 2004 daab
cologne london new york

published and distributed worldwide by
daab gmbh
stadtwaldgürtel 57
d - 50935 köln

p +49-221-94 10 740
f +49-221-94 10 741

mail@daab-online.de
www.daab-online.de

publisher ralf daab
rdaab@daab-online.de

art director feyyaz
mail@feyyaz.com

editorial project by loft publications
copyright © 2004 loft publications

editor Llorenç Bonet

layout Emma Termes
english translation Mathew Clarke
french translation Michel Ficerai
italian translation Grazia Suffriti
german translation Ulrike Fiedler
copy editing Raquel Vicente Durán

printed in spain
Anman Gràfiques del Vallès, Spain
www.anman.com

isbn 3-937718-06-0
d.l.: B-41033-04

all rights reserved.
no part of this publication may be reproduced in any manner.